T0020157

— THE UNTOLD STORY OF —
LARRY ITLIONG
LABOR RIGHTS HERO

BY CRISTINA OXTRA

Consultant:
Dr. James Zarsadiaz
Associate Professor of History
Director of the Yuchengco Philippine Studies Program
University of San Francisco

CAPSTONE PRESS
a capstone imprint

Published by Capstone Press, an imprint of Capstone
1710 Roe Crest Drive, North Mankato, Minnesota 56003
capstonepub.com

Library of Congress Cataloging-in-Publication Data is available on
the Library of Congress website.

ISBN: 9781669004806 (hardcover)
ISBN: 9781669004752 (paperback)
ISBN: 9781669004769 (ebook PDF)

Summary: You may have read about Cesar Chavez's leadership in organizing
the well-known Delano Grape Strike and Boycott of the 1960s. But did you
know it began as a strike led by Larry Itliong? He was a Filipino American labor
organizer who also worked with grape pickers in California. Uncover Itliong's
powerful story and how it connects to Chavez's story.

Editorial Credits
Editor: Ericka Smith; Designer: Sarah Bennett; Media Researcher: Svetlana
Zhurkin; Production Specialist: Katy LaVigne

Image Credits
Alamy: Alpha Stock, 15, Glasshouse Images, 13, History and Art Collection,
8, Pictures Now, 14; Associated Press: 23, File/George Brich, 19, Harold Filan,
29; Getty Images: Alaric Yanos, 7, Bettmann, 21, 25, Cathy Murphy, 27, Corbis/
Gerald L. French, 20, Corbis/Ted Streshinsky, 22, Denver Post, 24; Library of
Congress: Prints and Photographs Division/U.S. Farm Security Administration,
9, 10, 11; Shutterstock: Julia Khimich (background), cover (right) and
throughout, Nadegda Rozova (background), cover (left) and throughout;
Wayne State University: Walter P. Reuther Library/Archives of Labor and Urban
Affairs, cover, 4, 17

Direct Quotation
Page 28, from *La Cooperativa Campesina de California* article, "La Voz
Spotlight: Larry Itliong," lacooperativa.org

TABLE OF CONTENTS

Words in **bold** are in the glossary.

A FORCE FOR CHANGE

On September 7, 1965, Larry Itliong's powerful voice boomed across the Filipino Community Hall in Delano, California. "I want those in favor to stand up with your hand raised," he told hundreds of Filipino workers.

Everyone stood up. They raised their hands. They had decided to **strike**.

This was the beginning of the Delano Grape Strike. It was one of the most important labor movements in United States history. Filipino and Mexican farmworkers in California took on the state's powerful agricultural industry. And they gained better pay and working conditions for thousands of farmworkers.

Mexican American labor rights activists Cesar Chavez and Dolores Huerta are often celebrated as the leaders of the strike. But it began with Larry Itliong. This is his story.

SEEDS OF A DREAM

Modesto "Larry" Dulay Itliong was born on October 25, 1913. He was born in San Nicolas in the Philippines. His parents were farmers. He was one of six children.

The Philippines was a U.S. **colony** at the time, so Itliong learned English in school. He was also told that the U.S. was a place where everyone had the same opportunities.

As a young man, Itliong wanted to become a lawyer. He wanted to fight for the rights of others and help the poor. But there was no high school in his village, so Itliong only attended school through the sixth grade.

In 1929, 15-year-old Itliong sailed to the U.S. He wanted to pursue his dream of going to college and becoming a lawyer.

The northern coast of the Philippines

FACT In 1898, when Filipinos were fighting Spain for their independence, the U. S. was also at war with Spain. The treaty that ended the war that year gave the U. S. control over the Philippines. Filipinos fought the U. S. for control of their country but were unsuccessful. Filipinos didn't gain their independence from the U.S. until 1946.

CHAPTER 2

A MIGRANT WORKER'S LIFE

Itliong arrived in Seattle, Washington, on April 6, 1929. There, he met Filipino farmworkers. They were called the Manongs. They harvested crops along the West Coast. They also canned salmon in Alaska.

The Manongs did backbreaking work. They worked long hours in harsh conditions. But they could barely live on their **wages.**

Workers at a salmon cannery in Alaska

The Manongs

Larry Itliong was part of the Manongs—"elder brothers" in the Ilocano language of the Philippines. They were the generation of Filipinos who immigrated to the United States in the 1920s and 1930s. About 90 percent of the Filipino immigrants at the time were men. Motivated by the idea of the American Dream, the Manongs were a source of cheap labor for companies in the U.S. They came in search of opportunities but often found hardship and racism. Since interracial marriage was illegal in California until 1948, many remained single and did not have families.

A Filipino farmworker in California in the 1930s

A farmworker on a sugar beet farm in Montana

Itliong later headed to Montana. He worked the sugar beet harvest with other Filipinos. In the fields, workers had no access to clean drinking water or toilets. They slept in barns and other buildings that had dirt floors.

FACT In Montana, Itliong also worked on the railroad. While working, the fingers on his right hand got caught in a train door. Three of his fingers had to be removed, but that didn't slow him down. It earned him the nickname "Seven Fingers."

Itliong returned to Washington. He got a job as a janitor at a lettuce farm. The workers there went on strike to demand better wages and working conditions. Filipinos, including Itliong, joined the strike.

The strike lasted three weeks. White workers received a 10-cent raise and went back to work. Filipino workers did not receive a raise. Instead, they were replaced.

Filipino workers harvesting lettuce

Itliong moved again. He followed the work across California and Alaska with other Filipino **migrant** workers. Itliong struggled to survive. He also continued to witness farmworkers receive low wages, work in poor conditions, and have no protection against **pesticides.**

When he returned to Alaska, he joined the Filipino **cannery** workers' **union**. He wanted to help advocate for better pay and working conditions.

During the Great Depression of the 1930s, millions lost their jobs. Some blamed immigrants and migrants. They were violent toward them. While Itliong was in the Filipino part of town in Stockton, California, he saw a group of white teenagers beat up Filipinos. He also heard about other Filipinos being beaten or killed.

Anti-Filipino Laws

In 1934, the Tydings-McDuffie Act—which established a plan for the Philippines to become an independent nation—changed Filipinos' status from "national" to "alien." This meant that the U.S. could limit Filipino immigration to only 50 Filipinos per year. In 1935, the Filipino Repatriation Act offered Filipinos a one-way ticket back to the Philippines, but required that they never return. Other laws kept Filipinos from becoming U.S. citizens, voting, owning land, and marrying white people.

President Franklin D. Roosevelt signing the Tydings-McDuffie Act

SOWING SOLIDARITY

During World War II, Itliong served as a **messman** on a ship. Afterward, he settled in Stockton. When Filipinos were allowed to become U.S. citizens in 1946, he did. He also got married.

Stockton, California, in the 1950s

A camp for workers on an asparagus farm in California

In 1948, farmworkers who were harvesting asparagus in Stockton went on strike. A Filipino organizer and other union leaders were arrested. The government tried to **deport** one of them. This scared other Filipino organizers, so the farm labor movement slowed down.

In 1959, Itliong joined the Agricultural Workers Organizing Committee (AWOC). He recruited more than 1,000 new members. Then, he moved to Delano, California, to lead the Filipino grape workers there.

In 1965, grape growers in Delano refused to pay Filipino workers the same wages they had earned harvesting grapes in the Coachella Valley. Itliong asked AWOC members and the growers to meet on September 7. The growers didn't come to the meeting. So Itliong called on AWOC farmworkers to strike. Everyone agreed.

On September 8, led by Itliong, the Delano Grape Strike started. AWOC farmworkers walked off vineyards. They wanted a wage of $1.40 per hour, 25 cents for each box they packed, and the right to form a union.

The growers hired armed guards. They beat the strikers. They shot at them. They kicked them out of their camps. They shut off the power and water to their bunkhouses. They also hired Mexican workers to replace Filipino strikers.

A Filipino worker on the picket line in 1966 during
the Delano Grape Strike

FACT When the Delano Grape Strike began in 1965,
the Manongs were getting older. Many had not been
able to marry, so they had no families to care for them.
They needed better pay to help take care of themselves.

But Itliong didn't let that stop him. "I'm not scared of nobody," he said.

For years, the growers had **pitted** Filipino and Mexican workers against each other. They were separated in the fields. They lived in separate camps. And they were paid different wages.

Itliong believed Filipinos and Mexicans should work together. They would be more powerful and could take on the growers. He reached out to Dolores Huerta and Cesar Chavez. They were the leaders of the National Farm Workers Association (NFWA), another group in Delano. It was made up mostly of Mexican workers.

Itliong asked the NFWA to join the strike. Chavez wanted to wait. He didn't think the NFWA was ready for a strike. But Itliong urged him to join.

Cesar Chavez

On September 16, 1965, the NFWA voted to join the strike. Filipino Community Hall became the gathering place for Filipino and Mexican workers. They talked, ate meals together, and showed support for one another.

In 1966, the AWOC and the NFWA officially joined together. They created the United Farm Workers Organizing Committee (UFWOC). Chavez became its director. Itliong became its assistant director.

Itliong (center) and Chavez (right) marching in San Francisco in 1966

Bringing Attention to the Farmworkers' Movement

When the AWOC and the NFWA joined forces, they used many tactics to support their cause. They organized not just strikes, but marches and boycotts too. Chavez also fasted to encourage the strikers to stay committed to nonviolent tactics and to draw attention to their cause.

Their tactics worked. They received support across the country and around the world—from everyday people, civil rights activists, and lawmakers. But the attention was often on the charismatic, mild-mannered Chavez and not the tough, street-smart Itliong. Dr. Martin Luther King Jr. sent Chavez encouraging messages. Senator Robert Kennedy visited Chavez twice. The attention helped the farmworkers' movement, but it also centered Mexican farmworkers.

Senator Kennedy's visit with Chavez in 1968

CHAPTER 4

A GROWING MOVEMENT

The workers' strike would last five years. They also used other **tactics** to bring attention to their cause and pressure the grape growers to **negotiate** with them.

On March 17, 1966, the strikers began their march of more than 300 miles from Delano to the state capitol in Sacramento. As they passed through communities, they were joined by student activists, union organizers, civil rights workers, and religious leaders who supported them. When they reached the capitol on April 10, they were greeted by thousands of cheering people.

A grape field in Delano, California, with no workers during the strike

Strikers and their supporters at California's capitol building in Sacramento in 1966

That same year, Itliong and other UFWOC members traveled across the country. They asked people and grocery stores to **boycott** grapes from Delano grape growers.

Organizers signing contracts with grape growers in 1970

Finally, in 1970, more than two dozen Delano grape growers met with the UFWOC. They agreed to increase the farmworkers' pay and to provide health insurance. They also agreed to better control their use of pesticides. Victory at last!

But much of the progress the union made after the strike and boycott mostly benefited Mexican farmworkers. Filipinos felt left out whenever decisions were made. They started to leave the union. Itliong was also upset at the lack of support for the aging Manongs. He resigned from the UFWOC in 1971.

THE FRUITS OF HIS LABOR

After leaving the UFWOC, Itliong continued to advocate for Filipino farmworkers. As part of the agreement with the grape growers, a percentage of each box picked would support a retirement community for the Manongs. Itliong worked with Philip Vera Cruz to build it. They called it the Paolo Agbayani Village in honor of a Filipino farmworker who died during the strike. It opened in 1974.

Itliong supported other groups too. He helped create California Rural Legal Assistance. It provided legal assistance to low-income people. He organized farmworkers in Brazil and Chile. And he helped plan a strike against Safeway supermarkets.

A Filipino resident of the Agbayani Village in 1975

Decades later, Itliong's work started to receive the recognition it deserves. That's thanks to the efforts of a new generation of Filipino leaders.

In 2013, California's first Filipino state assemblyman Rob Bonta helped pass a bill that required public schools to teach Itliong's contributions to the farmworkers' movement.

In 2015, October 25 was declared Larry Itliong Day in California. And a school in Union City, California, was renamed Itliong-Vera Cruz Middle School.

On October 12, 2021, Itliong was inducted into the California Hall of Fame for his leadership in the labor movement.

Even though Itliong did not become a lawyer, he found a way to help others. He played a key role in the farmworkers' movement in the 1960s—one that has had a lasting impact on the collective power of farmworkers. "These men and women [farmworkers] put food on all of our tables working in some of the most difficult and backbreaking conditions. Itliong helped give these workers a powerful voice," said Bonta of Itliong's legacy.

Larry Itliong, 1967

GLOSSARY

boycott (BOY-kot)—to refuse to buy or use a product or service to protest something believed to be wrong or unfair

cannery (KAN-uh-ree)—a factory where food is put into cans

colony (KAH-lun-ee)—a country or area under the control of another country

deport (di-PORT)—to send people back to their country of origin

messman (MESS-man)—an individual in the Navy who serves food and clears tables

migrant (MYE-gruhnt)—a person who moves from one place to another to find work or better living conditions

negotiate (ni-GOH-shee-ate)—to bargain or discuss something to come to an agreement

pesticide (PES-tuh-side)—a poisonous chemical used to kill insects, rats, and fungi that can damage plants

pit (PIT)—to create a rivalry between

strike (STRIKE)—to refuse to work because of a disagreement with an employer over wages or working conditions

tactic (TAK-tik)—an action planned to get specific results

union (YOON-yuhn)—an organized group of workers that tries to gain better pay, benefits, and working conditions

wage (WAJE)—the money an employer pays a worker

READ MORE

Mabalon, Dawn B. and Gayle Romasanta. *Journey for Justice: The Life of Larry Itliong.* Stockton, CA: Bridge and Delta Publishing, 2018.

Pulliam, Maxie Villavicencio. *Fierce Filipina: Inspired by the Life of Gliceria Marella de Villavicencio.* Self-published, 2021.

Tyner, Artika R. *The Untold Story of Sarah Keys Evans: Civil Rights Soldier.* North Mankato, MN: Capstone, 2023.

INTERNET SITES

Britannica Kids: Larry Itliong
kids.britannica.com/kids/article/Larry-Itliong/634086

Kiddle: Little Manilla, Stockton, California Facts for Kids
kids.kiddle.co/Little_Manila,_Stockton,_California

PBS: Delano Manongs
pbs.org/video/kvie-viewfinder-delano-manongs/

INDEX

ABOUT THE AUTHOR

Cristina Oxtra is a Filipino American author. She earned an MFA in creative writing for children and young adults at Hamline University. She received the 2019–2020 Mirrors & Windows Fellowship for Indigenous writers and writers of color at the Loft Literary Center. She lives in Minnesota, where she enjoys spending time with family, cooking, baking, martial arts, supernatural and paranormal TV shows, and comic cons. Her website is www.cristinaoxtra.com.